People Aren't Robots:

A practical guide to the psychology and technique of questionnaire design

F. Annie Pettit, PhD, FMRIA

Copyright © 2018 by F. Annie Pettit

Cover art by Dustin Holmes, DustinHolmes@Yahoo.com

All rights reserved. This book or any portion thereof may not be reproduced or used in any manner whatsoever without the express written permission of the publisher except for the use of brief quotations in a book review or scholarly journal.

All examples were conceived of by the author.

Second Printing: 2018
ISBN 978-1539730644
http://lovestats.ca

Dedicated to the millions of people
who kindly share their time and opinions to
help make our world a better place

People Aren't Robots

Table of Contents

Preface	5
Chapter 1: Get in the frame of mind	7
People aren't robots	7
People make mistaktes	7
People are basically good	8
People are busy	9
People have needs	9
People are biased	11
People first, researchers second	12
Chapter 2: General Techniques	14
General to specific	14
Use humanistic language	14
Shorten everything	15
Choose common	17
Be lenient with grammar	18
Use Your Manners	19
Have fun	19
Assume mobile only	20
Power to the people	21
Chapter 3: Screen for the right people	22
Category screener	22
Branded screener	25
Region screener	26
Market research screener	27
Screen out on more than extremes	28
How late is too late	29
Chapter 4: Screen for quality people	31
People having a bad day	31
People wanting the incentives	31
Data quality process	31
Data quality measures to use	33
Red herrings	33
Straightlining	33
Ranking	35
Sum question	35
Following instructions	35

Over click	36
Under click	36
Low incidence	36
High incidence	37
Open end length	37
Profanity	38
Gibberish	38
Open end satisficing	39
Speeding	39
Avoid using contradictions	40
Never use this question type	40

Chapter 5: Generic techniques — 42

KNOW WHAT A QUESTION IS	42
OPERATIONALIZE	42
PROVIDE AN OPT-OUT	43
START WITH THE IMPORTANT PART	44
RESPECT PEOPLE WHO ARE DISABLED	45
AVOID LEADING AND LOADED QUESTIONS	46
AVOID DOUBLE BARRELED QUESTIONS	46
AVOID REFERRING TO EARLIER ANSWERS	47
ORDER OF ANSWER OPTIONS	47
Alphabetical	47
Chronological	48
Randomized	48
Reverse ordered	49
STYLE OF ANSWER OPTIONS	49

Chapter 6: Question-specific techniques — 51

NUMERIC QUESTIONS	51
Start with a number	51
Include a zero	51
Include a maximum	52
Don't duplicate answers	53
Don't skip answers	53
Use intuitive breaks	53
Use common breaks	54
Play the misconstrue game	55
'Or' does not equal 'to'	56
Etc does not equal eg does not equal ie	57
Use your words	58
Request estimates	59
SINGLE-SELECTS/MULTI-SELECTS	60

SCALES	61
Scales don't reveal truth	61
Number of points	61
Balanced scales	61
Unbalanced scales	62
Midpoints	62
Scale labels	63
GRID/MATRIX QUESTIONS	64
Deconstruct grids	64
Choose few grid items	65
Create reverse keyed items	65
Create negative items	66
Instructions	66
RANK QUESTIONS	66
SUM QUESTIONS	67
OTHER (PLEASE SPECIFY)	67
SHORT TEXT	68
LONG TEXT	68

Chapter 7: Sensitive Questions — 69

DON'T ASSIGN NEGATIVITY	69
SOCIALLY UNDESIRABLE BEHAVIOURS	70
ILLEGAL ACTIVITIES	71

Chapter 8: Demographics — 72

GENDER/SEX	72
AGE	73
Matching words	73
People don't want to feel old	74
RACE/ETHNICITY	74
EDUCATION	75
EMPLOYMENT	75
CHILDREN	76

Chapter 9: Tidbits — 77

BRANDING A QUESTIONNAIRE	77
QUESTIONS PER PAGE	77
PRETESTING	77
EMAIL SUBJECT LINES	78
REMINDERS	79
REVEAL THE RESULTS	79

About the Author — 80

Preface

Questionnaire design is easy until you're faced with horrid data quality. The problem, as with most things, is that there is an art and science to designing an effective questionnaire. This book will guide you in a short, easy to read, and easy to follow format. How is it different from all the other questionnaire design books out there?

It gives practical advice from someone who has witnessed more than twenty years of good and poor choices that experienced and inexperienced questionnaire writers make. Yes, even academic, professional researchers make plenty of poor questionnaire design choices. Yes, even I make mistakes. I've seen every mistake in this book in live questionnaires.

It outlines how to design questions while keeping in mind that people are fallible, subjective, and emotional human beings. Not robots. It's about time someone did this, don't you think?

I hope that once you understand and apply these techniques, you too will hear people say "this is the best questionnaire I've ever answered!"

Chapter 1: Get in the frame of mind

Great questionnaires can only be created if you, the author, are in the right frame of mind. Yes, you must have a specific set of research goals written out and ready to be operationalized into specific questions but that's not what I'm referring to here.

I mean that you must be inquisitive, open-minded, and prepared to understand and appreciate the true nature of the human being who is about to tasked with completing your questionnaire. So let's get in the right frame of mind.

People aren't robots
First, researchers need to remember that people aren't respondents, they aren't participants, and they certainly aren't subjects. They are people. They experience a full set of emotions. They get happy, sad, and annoyed by insignificant things that happen to them and around them. They get frustrated with something today and then become pleased with it tomorrow. People get tired and bored and hangry.

As much as we'd like them to, people can't simply adjust their programming to access their unconscious minds. They aren't logical systems following precise algorithms. We need to stop expecting that people will sit down to a questionnaire and proceed through it as if they aren't dealing with the all the personal issues they struggled with today, yesterday, and all last year. People aren't robots.

People make mistaktes
I'm pleased to say that the typo in that title is precisely how I originally typed the title. Yup. I made mistake. I guarantee

there are more throughout this book even though I've proofread it many times. How many times have *you* found a typo in a report you wrote only after you'd given it to a client? When was the last time you forgot about a meeting or took a pen from a colleague's desk without realizing it? You're not perfect either. People make mistakes, misread, and misinterpret things. What that means is that there is no such thing as an error-free questionnaire or dataset.

If you need data that is less contaminated by memory loss and human interpretation, consider instead using loyalty data, shopper data, and purchase receipts. If you must know people's deepest, darkest emotions, consider instead biometric techniques such as implicit measurement, voice patterns, eye-tracking, and hypnosis to get closer to the unconscious mind. And yes, those data will also have errors. Because people aren't robots.

People are basically good
People regularly donate blood, hold doors open, shovel their neighbour's walkway, lead Girl Guide troops, say please, refill the photocopier, let someone else have the last cookie (I don't), and volunteer for their industry associations out of the kindness of their hearts.

People who decide to use their billable, available time to complete questionnaires genuinely value the opportunity to participate in the product and service development process. It makes them feel helpful, important, and that they're contributing to the greater good. Researchers must go through the questionnaire writing and data analysis process with the assumption that people are basically good.

People are busy
People have kiddies who want to play, chihuahuas that want to run around the dog park, and spouses who need a shoulder to rest on after a hard day. People need to check emails, play games, shovel snow, make dinner, apply for jobs, and binge-watch Netflix for ten hours straight without getting up from the couch except to confirm there's still nothing in the fridge.

People have literally thousands of other things to do that are vastly more important and interesting than clicking circles and boxes in your questionnaire. As much as you love your work and your project, your top-priority, rush job, highly important questionnaire comes pretty low on everyone else's priority list. And deservedly so.

People have needs
You've probably seen Maslow's Hierarchy of Needs. Whether you believe in it, it offers a way of thinking that is highly relevant to questionnaire design.

People have needs. At the lowest level of Maslow's hierarchy, people are dealing with physiological needs - fighting to stay alive, struggling to eat, sleep, clothe, and shelter themselves. Once people can do this, they are able to progress to the next level wherein they seek out safety – meeting their physiological needs without risking their lives to do so.

Imagine how people in these types of situations would answer a questionnaire. They would try extra hard to earn an incentive so they could use it to feed their family. They aren't lying when they deliberately give an incorrect answer. They're feeding their family.

The next level is love and belonging. People need to feel that they are a part of something. That they belong to something. That their opinions are important and useful. People can do this by demonstrating that they have the necessary knowledge and information required to participate in a survey. If that means rethinking or rationalizing how or when or why they buy a product, that also is not lying. That's simply meeting a human need for belonging.

After that comes the human need for esteem. People need to feel confident about themselves, that they have achieved something, that people respect them. Once again, think about this in the context of questionnaires. Some people feel that respect is earned through owning expensive cars, buying premium brands, or having more education and income. People struggling with esteem might feel they need to sway slightly from perfect truth to achieve esteem.

At the top of the hierarchy are self-actualized people. These people are content with who they are. They know they have strengths and weaknesses, and they accept and work with the fact that they have biases. Few people reach this stage as it's difficult to honestly accept and embrace your own flaws. This honesty includes admitting that you ate two bags of chips today, that you rarely brush your teeth, that you're 51 not 49 years old, and that you dropped out of college not because you chose to, but because you failed. It would be amazing if every person completing questionnaires was self-actualized, but that's not reality.

People are not designed to be precisely accurate and true to fact every second of every day. They have emotional and psychological needs that interfere with the facts.

Because, you know.... People aren't robots.

People are biased
The authors of these two websites have created beautiful posters available for purchase listing 24 and 180 cognitive biases (https://yourbias.is/, https://designhacks.co/). I suspect it's safe to say we haven't even discovered all the human biases yet.

Rather than spending hours working through every detail of every daily situation, people unconsciously take advantage of cognitive biases to make assumptions and save time. Here are just a few that impact people every single time they interact with a questionnaire.

Anchoring: Relying too much on the first piece of information we received to make a decision. In other words, relying on what we learned in Question 1 to answer Question 5.

Availability heuristic: Overestimating events that come to mind more readily for us. In other words, naming a specific brand we bought yesterday despite the fact we usually buy a different brand.

Bandwagon effect: Tendency to say things because other people say those things. In other words, using question introductions to figure out what your answer to a question should be.

Distinction bias: Tendency to view two things as more dissimilar when evaluating them together rather than separately. That's a description of conjoint research, isn't it!

And that's just four biases. It's impossible to account for every bias when creating a questionnaire. The best thing you can do is be aware that hundreds of cognitive biases exist and be ready for them to interfere with responses.

People first, researchers second

As you write your questionnaire, you will regularly focus on your own personal needs. You *need* to generate precise data, you *need* to know about these 14 brands, you *need* data for these 83 questions. Your focus is on creating data that your data analyst, your statistician, your report writer can spin into an amazing story. Your need for very specific pieces of data will lead you to create longer questionnaires, more complicated question wording, longer lists of answer options, and longer scales. Your need for data will lead to bad experiences for research participants.

Your mantra *must* be participants first, researchers second. Do not let your personal needs lead to horrible experiences for participants. Adhere to the techniques you'll soon read about as strictly as you can. Fight for better participant experiences using these techniques so that people will want to continue sharing their experiences in the future.

People aren't robots.

Chapter 2: General Techniques

General to specific
There are always exceptions to the rule and only an experienced, trained researcher can help you in this regard. However, a good general rule is that questionnaires should begin as general as possible and gradually become more specific.

For example, begin by asking about a variety of products. Then ask about food products. Then ask about breakfast products. Then ask about hot breakfast products.

Similarly, begin by asking what they like and dislike about a product. Then prompt them with questions about shape, size, or colour. Then specifically ask about the green colour.

The strategy should always be to reveal as little as you possibly can until you absolutely cannot avoid naming the thing anymore. The goal is to let people discover and reveal their opinions along way rather than feed and lead impressions and opinions along the way.

Use humanistic language
The questionnaire design industry has a history of using precise and professional language, detailed questions, lengthy answers, and essay style introductions and descriptions such as you might see during the era of Charles Dickens and Virginia Woolf when single sentences stuffed with long, pretentious words, and elegant flowing phrases easily filled an entire page. This must stop.

Shorten everything

There is no right answer to the questionnaire length problem. Some researchers argue that any length is a good length as long as people are appropriately compensated. Other researchers will offer detailed tables and graphs illustrating the decline of data quality as questionnaires lengthen, particularly after ten and twenty minutes. As such, put your human-being costume on again and think about what real people are like.

Real people are interrupted by TV commercials every 7 minutes. Real people check Instagram and Snapchat every 3 minutes. Real people have a hard time staying on task even when they're doing something they love.

With that in mind, aim for questionnaires of ten minutes or less. Occasionally a longer questionnaire will be necessary and that's okay. Reward people appropriately, treat them respectfully, and then go back to ten-minute questionnaires.

There are easy ways to shorten questionnaires and that includes using fewer questions, shorter questions, shorter answer options, shorter descriptions, and shorter instructions.

Traditional: *Which of these categories best describes the region in which you live?*
Better: *Where do you live?*

Cut questions you won't use. Review every question and truly consider whether you will implement real change based on the results. If you *know* you won't change the brand colour, update the tagline, drop a SKU, decrease the price, or pick a different celebrity endorser then don't waste people's time asking about those things.

Remove the rambling additional information you inserted to organize your own thoughts rather than help the person reading the questionnaire.

Cut unnecessary instructions such as 'Please select one' particularly when it is impossible to select two, or when the question implies the number of required answers. You can often reword questions to include instructions thereby negating the need for additional, lengthier instructions.

Traditional: *Which of these best describes you? (Please select one answer)*
Better: *Which ONE of these best describes you?*

Traditional: *Choose the options that you look for when buying cereal. (Please select two answers from the following list)*
Better: *Choose the TWO options that you look for when buying cereal.*

Traditional: *Which features do you like? (Please select all that apply from this list.)*
Better: *Please select ALL the features that you like.*

When examples are necessary, shorten the questions and put the examples after the question on a separate line. Don't stuff the sentence. But first, consider whether people truly need those examples and reminders.

Traditional: *How often do you buy beverages at convenience stores (for example, juice, soda, water, coffee)?*

Better: *How often do you buy beverages at convenience stores?*
(e.g., juice, soda, water, coffee)

Best: *How often do you buy beverages at convenience stores?*

Ask about fewer concepts. Asking people the same set of questions about two concepts is ok but asking them to do this for three or more concepts encourages boredom and poor quality data. Consider shortening the questionnaire by having each person share opinions about only two randomly selected concepts. Your statistician can piece the data back together afterwards.

Choose common
Avoid professional, arrogant, and marketing language. Choose words you would use if you were having a casual conversation with your friends.

Don't ask people where they 'purchase products' when you would ask your friends where they 'buy things.' Don't ask if they 'use coffee' or 'consume coffee' when you would ask your friends if they 'drink coffee.' Don't ask if they 'utilize products' when you'd ask your friend if they 'use products.' Don't ask people about 'Proposition 19' if your friends talk about the 'marijuana legalization proposition.'

Ignore category labels, product descriptions, and technical jargon used around the office. Choose words used by average people going about their daily business.

Don't write 'MNC' instead of multi-national corporation, or 'CPG' instead of consumer-packaged goods or 'PC' instead of personal computer. It might take more space, but you're better off using clear words like 'companies with offices around the world' and 'products that people use every day'.

Statistics Canada reports that only about 25% of people have a university degree. Chances are you have a university degree and your writing style reflects that. You need to make sure your language is understandable by people who finished their formal education at high school, or people who speak English as a second language (20% of Canadians!).

If your target group has above average reading skills, for instance professional people such as psychologists or engineers, it's okay to use more complicated wording and grammar. But if you aren't certain, write questions with a grade 9 or 10 reading level.

A quick online search for 'reading level calculator' will give you tools to assess the reading level of questionnaires. If the readability score is over Grade 9, rewrite your questions.

Write for the people who will answer the questionnaire, not for the people who will create, analyze, and interpret it.

Be lenient with grammar
Questionnaires are not the place to enforce perfect grammar. It is okay to say things like 'Thanks a bunch' or 'You've been a big help. Thanks!' And, it is even okay to start a sentence with 'And,' or end it with a preposition such as 'of.' The goal is to make people feel comfortable with the language, ensure they understand the questions, and help them find an answer that accurately reflects their opinion.

Which of these groups do you belong to?
Who do you buy cold cereal for?
And, who do you buy hot cereal for?
What types of cars are you interested in?
When it comes to health care, what are you most concerned about?

Further, capital letters mean something. Do not strew them around because the word describes the category you're working with or it's a noun. Capital letters are for proper nouns like people's names, brand names, company names, and the beginning of sentences. (And, of course, for clarity as in the above example where ONE is all capital letters.)

Incorrect: *Which of these Daily Moisturizing Lotions have you tried?*
Correct: *Which of these daily moisturizing lotions have you tried?*

Use Your Manners

Maybe it's the Canadian in me, but friends use courtesy words like 'please,' 'thank you,' 'pardon me,' 'I'm sorry,' and 'if you don't mind' when they speak with you. It's part of the social contract people agree to when communicating with others. Carry that social contract into your questionnaire design.

Begin and end each questionnaire with words of politeness. Use courtesy words throughout, not so much that it becomes nauseating, but enough that people see you genuinely respect the time and effort they put in to helping you.

Thank you for agreeing to participate in this research.
Thank you in advance for your time and effort.
You're half way there! Thanks so much!
We greatly appreciate the time and effort you took to complete this questionnaire.

Have fun

Consider using occasional, light humour. That doesn't mean cramming knock-knock jokes and cartoons in between every question, and it certainly doesn't mean including political, religious, or off-colour jokes. Aim instead for encouraging and relevant humour.

This might not be as fun as a cat video, but we hope you enjoy answering our questionnaire!
May the survey force be with you!
This part might a bit boring, but we know you can do it!
Woo hoo! You're halfway done!

By the way, this is my favourite joke.

What's worse than a pie chart?
Two pie charts!
(Alternatively, a 3D pie chart!)

Assume mobile only

Assume that a tiny mobile phone is the only place people will complete your questionnaire. As internet access increases globally and spreads to more unusual places like underground transportation and remote areas, more and more people will answer questionnaires on small devices. Right now, at least 30% of questionnaires are answered on small devices and this number will only increase.

Researchers need to write questionnaires that are readable, understandable, and answerable without scrolling and pinching on tiny screens. Short questions and short answers are the only option.

Further, many people are bound by wireless contracts and service plans that make downloading images and video personally expensive. Some people even set their small devices to prevent high bandwidth items from downloading.

Unless it is essential for the research, don't include images, sounds, videos, and extraneous features. And if you must use these items, tell people beforehand that they are forthcoming, and use technology to only offer those features to devices that can handle them.

Power to the people

The last question of every questionnaire should always be an optional, open end verbatim. For the entire survey, you, the researcher, were in charge. You dictated every topic and every answer. You constrained every answer and limited every topic. You bossed people around. Now it's time to give power to the people.

Give people an open space to expand on their answers, provide answers to questions you didn't ask about, or complain about how terrible your survey was. Read these comments and take them to heart. Learn for the next time.

Is there anything else you would like to share about this topic or the survey itself? (Optional)

Chapter 3: Screen for the right people

Let's return to our principle wherein we realize that people are not robots. People have an inherent need to belong, to contribute, to be a part of something bigger than themselves, and this includes being part of the survey process. People want to share their thoughts and opinions like everyone else is.

Even when it's obvious that someone's demographic or psychographic criteria do not meet the targeting strategy, their knowledge and experience might convince them that they ought to complete the questionnaire. Researchers might see this slight fudging of answers to participate in a survey as lying but that is simply not the case. People are doing their best to help you find a person who knows about the topic. Themselves. Fortunately, you have techniques to minimize this problem.

Category screener
Begin questionnaires with a well-designed, broad category screener. In this (bad) example, readers can tell that the questionnaire will be about daily moisturizing lotion.

Traditional: Do you currently use daily moisturizing lotion?
- *Yes*
- *No*

Someone who no longer uses lotion but has a lot of experience and knowledge with the category might choose 'Yes' because they feel they know enough about the category to provide valid answers. Someone who is responsible for the personal care of another person who currently uses lotion would also have a lot of experience with and knowledge about the topic. Of course, we know that if those people were the target group, the screening question would have been phrased differently. Those people are not our target audience.

Even worse, there will always be a few people who want to qualify for the incentive. These people will be able to tell from this question that they must answer 'yes' to qualify and complete the questionnaire. Consequently, the yes/no, dichotomous format is a poor question type and shouldn't be used if it can be avoided. Indeed, the yes/no format is frequently best avoided altogether in questionnaires.

Fortunately, you can decrease the likelihood of leading people to respond in this specific way. Begin with a broad category question that meets several criteria.

First, include common answer options that nearly every person completing the questionnaire will be able to choose. Give every person a way to belong to the survey, to see that they can participate and share their answers.

Second, include at least two unusual answer options that almost nobody will select. These answer options will allow you to identify people who are trying to qualify for the survey. Disqualify from the survey anyone who chooses *two or more* of these unusual items. Try to include unusual answers that reflect a variety of categories, e.g., food, beverage, pharmaceutical, personal care, pet care, home care. We do risk disqualifying a few good people, but it is more important to avoid poor quality data.

Third, include several detractors that mirror the target answer in both character length and uniqueness. If the target answer is particularly long or short, then the detractors should be particularly long or short. If the target answer has several examples or is unusually specific, then so should the detractors. Once again, the detractors should reflect a broad set of categories.

In the following example, the research is about a daily moisturizing lotion branded as HealthyHands. The questionnaire does not begin with a binary/dichotomous question about whether the person uses HealthyHands. Instead, it begins with a generic category question that can identify people who use the target category. This example has 8 answer options reflecting 7 different categories. If someone didn't know the questionnaire was about lotion, it would be impossible for them to pinpoint the qualifying answer and be 'helpful.' Similarly, it's impossible to tell which community service is the 'correct' answer in the second example.

Which of these products have you used in the last 12 months?
- ☐ *Adult diapers for men* [Detractor]
- ☐ *Ambergris seasoning* [Unusual]
- ☐ *Cooking oil* [Common]
- ☐ *Daily moisturizing lotion* [Target group]
- ☐ *Dryer sheets* [Common]
- ☐ *Deodorant paste* [Unusual]
- ☐ *Unbleached paper towels* [Detractor]
- ☐ *None of these*

Which of these services have you used in the last 12 months?
- ☐ *Community fitness centre*
- ☐ *Day care services*
- ☐ *Drivers licence office*
- ☐ *Immigration and newcomer services*
- ☐ *In-home health care services*
- ☐ *Mental health services*
- ☐ *Public library*
- ☐ *None of these*

Branded screener

After this category question, the next screener question should be a branded question. The strategy is similar to the first screener question. The answer options should include the target answer, two or three common answers, and two or three rare answers.

In addition, the most important feature of this question is the inclusion of two or three red herrings, answers that do not exist as confirmed through a careful internet search. Do not trust yourself to create answers that don't exist. Do an internet search to ensure that the made-up brands, products, or services aren't real things that you've simply not heard of. On *many* occasions, I've invented fake brand names that turned out to be real.

The following example includes eight answer options. Notice that the red herrings aren't together, nor are the common brands, nor the rare brands. None of the brands stand out as more or less obvious than the others. Once again, it is impossible for a reader to know which brand is the target answer that will qualify them for an incentive. There doesn't appear to be a 'correct' answer. Similarly, it is impossible to know what the 'correct' organization in the second example is.

Before now, which of these brands of daily moisturizing lotion had you heard of?

- ☐ Aveeno — *[Common brand]*
- ☐ Dermatolin — *[Red herring]*
- ☐ HealthyHands — *[Target group]*
- ☐ Hope In A Jar — *[Rare brand]*
- ☐ Jergens — *[Common brand]*
- ☐ Sebamed — *[Rare brand]*
- ☐ Sensitin — *[Red herring]*
- ☐ None of these

Before today, which of these organizations had you heard of?
- ☐ *Doctors Without Borders*
- ☐ *Greenpeace*
- ☐ *Kiva*
- ☐ *Last Chance at Life*
- ☐ *Save the Children*
- ☐ *Wave-OH!*
- ☐ *World Wildlife Fund*
- ☐ *None of these*

Questionnaires may require several more screener questions to adequately reflect all the necessary criteria but the essence is the same. Start broad and general, and gradually get more specific. Do not reveal the survey topic until you have no other choice. And, provide appropriate alternative answers so that everyone can feel that they belong by giving substantive answers. This applies to the entire questionnaire, not just the screener section.

Region screener

When using a client list or research panel, you know where people live because they completed the profiling or establishment survey within the last 12 months. However, people move regularly enough, particularly young adults, that it makes sense to ask again at the beginning of a questionnaire. As with many questions, it's easy to offer a binary yes/no screening question but we've already learned this is a bad idea. It's obvious that the target group of this question is people who live in the USA.

Traditional: Do you live in the United States of America?
- ○ *Yes*
- ○ *No*

Instead, offer people a region question that includes a choice of reasonable options. If the target group is people who live in the USA, offer a range of other English-speaking countries. If the target group is a specific city, offer similarly populous or non-populous options.

Where do you live?
- ○ *Australia*
- ○ *Canada*
- ○ *United Kingdom*
- ○ *United States*
- ○ *Other*

Where do you live?
- ○ *Calgary*
- ○ *Edmonton*
- ○ *Ottawa*
- ○ *Montreal*
- ○ *Toronto*
- ○ *Winnipeg*
- ○ *Other*

Market research screener

Consumer questionnaires often screen out people who work in the marketing, research, and advertising industries. It's not necessarily a bad thing to do but it is worth reconsidering.

First, researchers recognize this question and know how to answer it so they won't be disqualified. That nonsense aside, researchers complete questionnaires because they love questionnaires. They do it because they want to see the work of other researchers and improve upon their own questionnaire writing skills. They are NOT doing competitive research and snooping out the innovations of other brands. They'd have to waste hundreds of hours answering hundreds of surveys before finding one that was snoop-worthy.

Second, market researchers and advertisers pine for and buy as many products and services as other people. Their shopping behaviors are as emotional, unreasonable, and illogical as everyone else's, and their opinions are as valid as everyone else's. It makes more sense to include them in the research unless there is a genuinely logical reason to exclude them. Researchers are not robots.

Screen out on more than extremes

People who regularly complete questionnaires know how screeners work. If you're the person who has the lowest income or the highest education or if you've bought the fewest boxes of something, you're the person who will be screened out. As such, make sure that screener questions based on rankings, frequencies, or numbers give people room for a bit of exaggeration so that even if they deliberately avoid the extreme answer, they will be properly screened in or out.

In this example, the target group might only include people who are aged 18 years and older. By starting with a '17 or under' option, someone who is 17 but will turn 18 next month might say that they are 18 so they won't be screened out. By splitting out the younger ages, it is no longer clear what the 'right' answer is. Indeed, it now appears the 'right' answer might be a teenager. The chances of a 17-year-old fudging their answer to be 18 will be lessened.

Traditional: *What is your age?*
     o   *17 or under*
     o   *18 to 29*
     o   *39 to 49*
     o   *50 to 69*
     o   *70 or over*

Better: *What is your age?*
- *12 or under*
- *13 to 15*
- *16 to 17*
- *18 to 29*
- *39 to 49*
- *50 to 69*
- *70 or over*

Similarly, the following example highlights how someone might be inappropriately screened in as a decision maker when all they've done is offer one or two opinions at work. By adding more detailed answer options, people have more ways to explain their relevant experience, and the right group of people can be properly screened in and out of the research.

Traditional: *How much responsibility do you have for buying electronic equipment at work?*
- *I make the decision by myself*
- *I have input into the decision*
- *I am not involved in those decisions*

Better: *How much responsibility do you have for buying electronic equipment at work?*
- *I make the decision by myself*
- *I share the decision with someone else*
- *I provide input or research into the decision*
- *I offer advice when asked about those decisions*
- *I have no responsibility for those decisions*

How late is too late

It's expensive to give full incentives to every person who begins a questionnaire but does not meet the research needs to complete it. It is also disrespectful to expect people to complete several minutes of a questionnaire and then not compensate them because they 'did not qualify.' The fact that they did not quality is *your* problem. They accepted your invitation with the intention of completing the questionnaire and you reneged on the offer.

As such, avoid screening people out once they have answered more than 5% or 10% of the questionnaire. If there is no alternative, find a way to offer them a small thank you incentive. The incentive is not a thank you just for today. It's an incentive for them to participate in the future as well.

Chapter 4: Screen for quality people

The token gifts offered for completing questionnaires aren't much incentive for spending time falsifying data. The good thing is that most people feel rewarded, at least in part, by knowing they've helped to create better products and services. However, two types of people can be problematic.

People having a bad day
Even the best of us have difficulty paying attention and make a few mistakes sometimes. I make lots of mistakes and I'm willing to bet there is at least one typo, likely several, in this book. It's not fair to penalize people for being human and making mistakes, being tired, or becoming bored. Of course, if someone is having a bad day or is having a lot of trouble concentrating *right now*, they shouldn't complete your questionnaire. Maybe tomorrow, but not now. Questionnaire techniques need to screen out people who are having a bad day today.

People wanting the incentives
Although most people are basically good, there will always be a few people who are in it for the incentives. Some of these people will say anything to get a small incentive, perhaps lie, perhaps answer with random responses. Fortunately, you've got techniques in hand right now to help screen out people who are deliberately creating low quality and invalid data.

Data quality process
If a questionnaire is closer to ten minutes, many of these techniques can be applied to your existing questions. A shorter questionnaire might require the addition of two or three questions.

The basic process is as follows:

☆ Insert at least three different measures in three different locations of the questionnaire. I normally include at least 10 and sometimes up to 15 different checks. I'm not exaggerating. More is often better as long as the length of the questionnaire is not increased unnecessarily.

☆ After data collection, using a point system, count the number of measures failed in each completed questionnaire. The final score for each complete could range from 0 to 15 depending on how failures are assigned. Few completes will generate a score of 0 or make no errors. This is a perfect reminder that making an error does *not* mean someone is a poor participant. It simply means someone is behaving in a way that the questionnaire writer did not plan for. You should rethink how you wrote that question the next time you field it.

☆ Identify the 5% of completes with the highest scores. These completes will include both good participants having a bad day, as well as a few participants deliberately creating poor data.

☆ Remove these 5% of completes from the data file and conduct the analyses as if those completes did not exist. In other words, plan from day one to include an extra 5% in your sample size. (If you're a data geek, run some side by side tables and look at how different that data is! It's fascinating!)

☆ If a research panel is used, send the UserIDs of those 5% of people to the panel team. A good quality panel will track which panelists are habitual poor performers and ban them from future projects.

Data quality measures to use

The goal with each measure is to label about 5% of completes as demonstrating a poor quality behaviour. If one of the measures flags 20% or more of the completes, there are a couple of options.

First, ignore the measure because it identified a normal behaviour, not an aberrant behaviour. The goal is not to penalize people acting normally.

Second, leave the measure as is. This option is feasible if you're using many different data quality measures such that this one will not have an unreasonable influence on the results. If it is only one of ten measures, those 20% of people will only be penalized if they demonstrate several other problematic behaviours as well.

The goal of these measures is not to identify psychic robots that can read and interpret everything exactly as you intended. The goal is to identify people who've made so many mistakes that they probably did not pay attention to the questions - today.

Red herrings

As part of a multi-select or Check-All-That-Apply question type, create two or three brands, products, or names that sound valid but do not exist. Check each one with an internet search because made-up brands or people are often real names you weren't aware of. To account for poorly conceived red herrings, only flag completes that have *two or more* red herrings selected.

Straightlining

As a general concept, straightlining refers to more than simply selecting the same answer for every item in a grid (e.g., selecting 2 or Somewhat Agree for five grid items in a row). It can also refer to unlikely response patterns such as 1, 2, 3, 4, 5, or 1, 2, 1, 2, 1. These alternate patterns require either automated algorithms or a human eye to hunt them out but they are worthy of being flagged.

Traditional straightlining is easily identified by calculating the standard deviation of responses to a grid question. Regardless of what the mean (average) score of a set of grid items is, if the standard deviation is 0, straightlining has occurred. Also consider standard deviations less than 0.5 as this will identify completes that *nearly* straightlined. Flag each occurrence.

Straightlining can *not* be measured on poorly designed grid questions. In the following example, it is logical for someone to agree with every item, and good participants will straightline because you enabled it. People should not be penalized for your weak questionnaire design skills. This grid must be fixed before it can be used to measure straightlining (see Chapter 4: Grid questions).

Not appropriate for measuring straightlining:
What is your opinion about this breakfast cereal?

It tastes good	○	●	○	○	○
It is nutritious	○	●	○	○	○
It has a good variety of flavours	○	●	○	○	○
My kids like it	○	●	○	○	○
It is an affordable price	○	●	○	○	○

Better for measuring straightlining:
What is your opinion about this breakfast cereal?

It tastes awful	○	○	○	●	○
It is nutritious	○	●	○	○	○
It has a good variety of flavours	○	●	○	○	○
My kids like it	○	●	○	○	○
It is too expensive	○	●	○	○	○

Ranking

If a ranking question requires people to type numbers instead of dragging and dropping items into order, consider turning off automated validation. Let people rank order the answers as they wish. Include an instruction such as:

Please rank the following answers from 1 through 5. Use each number only once.

Any case where a number is used twice or a number greater than 5 or less than 1 is used receives a flag.

Sum question

If this measure is used, recognize that questionnaires are not math tests and that math makes some people anxious. Leniency is required.

Like ranking, this measure only works when automated validation is not used. It won't work if people are technically not permitted to provide answers that do not add up to the desired amount. Use an instruction such as the following:

Please make sure your numbers add up to 100%.

Assign a flag to any complete where the numbers add up to more than 105 or less than 95 (or another reasonable range where fewer than 5% of completes would be identified). The goal is to accept reasonable math, not perfect math.

Following instructions

This measure works well as part of a multi-select. Invite participants to choose a specific number of items from the list but do not validate the number. If you ask people to choose 3 items, allow them to choose any number of items. Make sure to do this in a situation where the specific number of selected items isn't essential for the validity of data analysis. Any complete that doesn't include the precise number of requested items receives a flag. The instruction could be as follows:

Please select the 3 features that are most important to you.

Over click
This measure applies to Multi-Select or Check-All-That-Apply questions. It works best when there are 8 to 20 items in a list. When people can choose as many or few options as they wish from a long list, the number of options chosen across a sample of people will form a type of normal distribution. Some people will choose many options, some few options, but most will choose a moderate number of options. Count the number of answer options selected by each complete, and then flag the 5% of completes with the highest number of selected options.

Under click
Similar to Over Click, this measure focuses on the 5% of completes with the fewest number of options selected in a Multi-Select. Flag these completes.

Low incidence
This measure applies to Multi-Select or Check-All-That-Apply questions. Include in the list of answer options at least two that are rare. Flag anyone who chooses two or more of the rare answer options. Possible answer options include:
◆ rare food ingredients
◆ rarely used medications
◆ rare diseases
◆ electronics that are far from being mainstream
◆ electronics that are out of date

- unusual hobbies
- rarely seen movies
- rarely read books

High incidence

Similar to Low Incidence, include two or more high incidence products. Flag any completes that do not select at least one of the high incidence items. Examples include:
- personal care products like toothpaste or toilet paper
- food products like bread or pasta
- beverages like coffee, water, or milk
- clothing such as socks or underwear
- ailments such as colds or headaches
- clothing such as pants or shirts

Open end length

The techniques described here can be handled easily and quickly using automated functions in spreadsheets or statistical software. As such, they can be run almost instantly on thousands of open ends. Reading and acting on the verbatims will come later.

Focus on open ends that everyone was required to answer in detail. Aim for questions that ask for a specific number of items to be named.

What three things do you like about television?
What three things do you like the most about your grocery store?
What one thing do you like about television, and what one thing do you dislike?

For such questions, it is impossible to provide a substantive answer using less than ten characters. Even an answer containing three weak ideas like 'fun yuk yay' requires 11 characters.

Flag any complete where the character count of the response is less than ten, or some other appropriately small number of characters.

To determine the length of a verbatim in cell A1 of Excel, the syntax is as follows:

> =LEN(A1)

Profanity
No matter how much you dislike it and refuse to use it, profanity is a normal part of everyday conversation. Words like damn, ass, or the 'F' word, are common expressions of anger and should not necessarily generate a flag. However, vastly worse profanity, which I'll leave nameless, should generate a flag. Save time by using syntax to search for these specific character strings.

To find a specific word, letter, or punctuation mark in cell AI of Excel, the syntax would be as follows:

> =FIND("damn",A1)

Gibberish
Use syntax to flag text characteristics that don't naturally occur in reasonable responses. These would be verbatims that:
◆ Do not include spaces
◆ Do not include vowels
◆ Contain certain double letters combinations such as qq, ww, yy, hh, jj, kk, zz, xx, vv, and bb. Take care to not penalize acronyms or brand names that might use them.
◆ Contain character strings that do not naturally occur, e.g., asdf, fjfjf, ghghg, qwer

You can search for non-use of spaces in Excel using the syntax:
> =FIND(" ",A1)

Open end satisficing

Someone who repeatedly does not give substantive answers is likely not taking care to think about their opinions. Set up a character search and assign a flag to any complete that uses any of these types of answers two or more times:
- *NA*
- *n.a.*
- *don't know*
- *dunno*
- *no idea*
- *no*
- *none*

Speeding

There is no right way to define speeding. A common definition is one third of the median time. For instance, if the median length of the questionnaire is ten minutes, anyone completing the questionnaire in less than one third of ten minutes would be classified as a speeder and receive a flag, i.e., less than 3.3 minutes.

My preferred option is not to define speeding until all the data is in hand. At that point, draw a cut-point at the fastest 5% of completion times. Those completes receive a flag worth one point. In addition, the fastest 2% of completes receive a second flag, also worth 1 point. The result is that the fastest 2% of people receive 2 points (2 flags) on the speeding measure. You might even decide to automatically exclude the fastest 2% of people.

Avoid using contradictions
Contradictions are a popular data quality measure but they regularly backfire. For instance, a pet owner might never buy pet food, a parent might never buy children's clothing, someone who hates milk might buy it every week, and someone who loves cereal might never eat it.

If a contradiction is used as a data quality measure, make sure it is one of many other measures. And, makes sure that you and several colleagues cannot think of any legitimate situations in which someone could perform the contradiction.

Never use this question type
Lastly, there is one data quality measure that should never be used. This is inserting a request to 'Choose option 2 for this item' or 'Select Strongly Agree here.'

Never use this measure: What is your opinion of this cereal?

Looks good	o	o	o	o	o
Delicious	o	o	o	o	o
Select the second answer	o	o	o	o	o
Expensive	o	o	o	o	o

There are several problems with this technique.

First, people think it is a mistake in the question, that the researcher forgot to finish something, and this makes researchers look silly and careless.

Second, some people might see it for what it is, that researchers do not trust people to complete questionnaires carefully. This perception, regardless of the reality, is disrespectful to people who are trying to do a good job.

Third, just as when a character in a movie talks to the camera (breaking the fourth wall), it jolts people out of their thought process.

Given that there are so many good alternatives, there is no reason to use this weak data quality measure.

Chapter 5: Generic techniques

Let's begin with recommendations that apply to many types of questions before focusing on specific questions.

Know what a question is
Statements end in periods. Questions end in question marks. Know the difference and use them properly.

Incorrect: *Please indicate which of the following apply to you?*
Correct: *Please indicate which of the following apply to you.*
Correct: *Which of the following apply to you?*

Incorrect: *Which ONE product do you use most frequently.*
Correct: *Select the ONE product you use most frequently.*
Correct: *Which ONE product do you use most frequently?*

Operationalize
Convert abstract constructs into their concrete, measurable components. People are hard-wired for cognitive biases that make them rationalize perceptions of constructs. However, we can mitigate some of the negative effects by focusing on concrete behaviours that are harder to misinterpret or rationalize.

Abstract concept
Do your practice good parenting skills?
   o *Yes*
   o *No*

Operationalized
In the last 4 weeks, which of these things have you done with your child?
   ☐ *Took them grocery shopping*
   ☐ *Asked them what they learned at school*
   ☐ *Took them to the library*
   ☐ *Picked them up from an after-school activity*
   ☐ *Told them a bedtime story*

Abstract concept
Do you value personal privacy?
- *Yes*
- *No*

Operationalized
In the last 6 months, which of these have you done?
- ☐ *Refused to provide my zip/postal code to a cashier*
- ☐ *Answered a personality quiz on Facebook*
- ☐ *Got an unlisted phone number*
- ☐ *Let a stranger use my cell phone*

Provide an opt-out

No matter how wonderful a questionnaire writer you are, you will rarely ever (never?) create the perfect question with the perfect answers that account for all possible world experiences. Therefore, aim to include one or more opt-out answers such as:

0
Do not buy/have/own/use any
Do not recall
Don't know
Never
None
None of the above
None of these
Not applicable
Other
Prefer not to answer

Keep in mind that 'None of these' or 'None of the above,' cannot be offered in combination with the 'Other' option. These are the *same* options. 'None of these' implies that the above options are not relevant, but a different option is relevant. In other words, an 'Other' option is relevant. If this is the case, consider if what you meant to use was 'Other' and 'Do not use':

Do not include both of these
- *None of these*
- *Other*

Instead, consider whether you actually mean this
- *Other*
- *Do not buy/have/own/use any*

Also, avoid lumping all the opt-out answers together into one 'Other/No opinion' answer. Create separate answers so that if many people choose the option, you'll know exactly why they have opted out of your answer choices and you'll be able to analyze the categories appropriately.

Incorrect:	*Other/Don't know*
Incorrect:	*Other/No opinion*
Incorrect:	*Other/Not applicable*
Correct:	*Other*
Correct:	*Don't know*
Correct:	*Not applicable*

Start with the important part

People may tune out before reading qualifiers placed at the end of a question. Instead, begin questions with the qualifiers, e.g., time frames such as last year, month, or week.

In just the last 2 weeks, how many times did you recommend HealthyHands to someone?

Thinking only about TV commercials, how many ads for HealthyHands have you seen?

Thinking only about the one grocery store you go to most often, how often do you buy HealthyHands there?

Including yourself, how many people live in your home?

Respect people who are disabled

As soon as you include colour, text, images, videos, or audio in a research project, you must ensure your questionnaire is accessible. You read that right. Every questionnaire should be accessible.

In this regard, recognize that people who are disabled use and buy products and services just like everybody does. They experience advertising and marketing like everybody does. Their experiences with your marketing materials may include accessibility devices and technology, but those experiences are valid, real world experiences. Make sure your questionnaire design accounts for this.

Colour blindness: If colour is an essential component of the questionnaire, search online for a colour-blindness checker to ensure the colours can be distinguished from each other.

Visual disabilities: Include narration of images and video.

Hearing disabilities: Include closed captioning or subtitles of audio and video.

Take care when prepping participants to review audio-visual materials. Unclear wording may screen out people simply because they have a disability. If someone usually experiences commercials with no sound or no visuals, that's no reason to exclude them from reviewing your materials with no sound or no visuals.

Traditional: Were you able to see and hear the video?
Better: Were you able to experience the video as you normally would?

Avoid leading and loaded questions

Rather than asking about agreement or importance, which may lead people to 'agree' with statements or say the statements are 'important', instead ask people to share their opinions. The scale wordings provide the framework for agreement and importance which makes restating those words unnecessary. Sometimes, this will even lead to shorter questions, a bonus outcome.

Traditional: *Do you strongly agree, somewhat agree, feel neutral, somewhat disagree, or strongly disagree with the following statements?*

Traditional: *How much do you agree or disagree with the following statements?*

Better: *What is your opinion about these statements?*

Incorrect: *Should parents who love their children purchase private health insurance?*

Correct: *Should parents purchase private health insurance for their children?*

Incorrect: *How amazing was our service?*
Incorrect: *How nice were our service representatives?*
Correct: *What is your opinion about our service?*

Incorrect: *Many people feel that health care should be a universal right for children. Are you also in favour of this?*

Correct: *What is your opinion about health care being a universal right for children?*

Avoid double barreled questions

Avoid incorporating two concepts into one question. Any time a question incorporates two nouns, two adjectives, two adverbs, or two anything, consider whether one of the words can be deleted or if the question ought to be split into two.

Incorrect: The cereal is tasty and healthy.
Correct: The cereal is tasty.
Correct: The cereal is healthy.

Incorrect: Is the company honestly transparent?
Correct: Is the company honest?
Correct: Is the company transparent?

Avoid referring to earlier answers

When people are reminded of something they said earlier in a questionnaire, it makes them question if they are being setting up to contradict themselves. In questionnaires, it is usually done with good intentions, to remind people about something they may have forgotten. But, if there is no need to remind someone of an earlier answer, don't. The benefit is a shorter question and no perceptions of mistrust.

Traditional: Earlier you said you didn't like HealthyHands. What in particular don't you like about it?
Better: What do you dislike about HealthyHands?

Traditional: Earlier you said you bought HealthyHands on your last grocery shopping trip. Why did you buy it?
Better: Why did you buy HealthyHands on your last grocery shopping trip?

Order of answer options

Answer options are often listed in the order they were thought of but there is usually a much better choice.

Alphabetical

Alphabetical lists are appropriate when people know what their answer is before they see the possible answers. This is the case for stores, brands, TV shows, or the names of famous people.

Where do you usually do your grocery shopping?
- ☐ *Great Canadian Superstore*
- ☐ *Loblaws*
- ☐ *Kroger*
- ☐ *Sobeys*
- ☐ *Walmart*
- ☐ *Zehrs*
- ☐ *Other*

Chronological

If the answers relate to time or processes, chronological order will work best. This includes days of the week, time of day (e.g., morning, afternoon, evening), and processes that must carried out in a specific order (e.g., baking requires one to list the ingredients, shop for the ingredients, mix together the ingredients, bake the cake, and eat the cake).

Which days do you usually go grocery shopping?
- ☐ *Monday*
- ☐ *Tuesday*
- ☐ *Wednesday*
- ☐ *Thursday*
- ☐ *Friday*
- ☐ *Saturday*
- ☐ *Sunday*

Randomized

Random order works best when there is no inherent order to the items such as a list of why people like something, or a list of product features.

What is your opinion about grocery shopping?
- ☐ *It's a chore I wish I didn't have to do*
- ☐ *I love finding new products*
- ☐ *It's a great way to relax*
- ☐ *I would love to never shop for groceries again*

Reverse ordered

Scales such as agreement or importance work well in reverse order. Across an entire questionnaire, consider randomizing whether a person will see all their scales beginning with the negative or positive phrasing.

For example, one person might see every scale in their questionnaire like this:

> *Agree strongly, Agree somewhat, Neutral, Disagree somewhat, Disagree strongly*

And, another person might see every scale in their questionnaire like this:

> *Disagree strongly, Disagree somewhat, Neutral, Agree somewhat, Agree strongly*

Style of answer options

When building lists of phrases for answer options, ensure that every option uses the same type of phrase. For instance, every phrase in a list should begin with a noun, or a verb, preferable an active verb.

Incorrect: *In the last 7 days, which of these activities did you do?*
- ☐ *Swim*
- ☐ *Biked*
- ☐ *Reading*

Correct: *In the last 7 days, which of these activities did you do?*
- ☐ *Swimming*
- ☐ *Biking*
- ☐ *Reading*

Incorrect: In the last 4 weeks, which of these did you do with your child?
☐ Take them grocery shopping
☐ We drive to school together
☐ Taking them to the library

Correct: In the last 4 weeks, which of these things have you done with your child?
☐ Took them grocery shopping
☐ Took them to school
☐ Took them to the library

Better: In the last 4 weeks, where did you take your child?
☐ Grocery store
☐ School
☐ Library

Chapter 6: Question-specific techniques

Numeric questions

Start with a number

Start each answer option with a number. Rather than say 'more than 9,' say '10 or more'. This allows people to quickly scan the first character in each line to see which answer applies to them.

Incorrect: *How many boxes of cereal are in your cupboard?*
- *0*
- *1 to 4*
- *5 to 9*
- *More than 9*

Correct: *How many boxes of cereal are in your cupboard?*
- *0*
- *1 to 4*
- *5 to 9*
- *10 or more*

Include a zero

Questionnaires often fail to include zeros because we assume those people were screened out in an earlier question. However, people occasionally make mistakes, misread, forget, or misinterpret things. Further, don't include 0 within the low volume answer option. Specifically include the zero.

Incorrect: *How many pairs of shoes do you own?*
- *1 to 4*
- *5 to 9*
- *10 or more*

Incorrect: How many pairs of shoes do you own?
- 4 or less
- 5 to 9
- 10 or more

Incorrect: How many pairs of shoes do you own?
- 0 to 4
- 5 to 9
- 10 or more

Correct: How many pairs of shoes do you own?
- 0
- 1 to 4
- 5 to 9
- 10 or more

Include a maximum

Along the same lines, even if the high volume or heavy users have been screened out, always include a maximum number. Even if the highest number seems improbable, don't end on '99.' If there is any possibility that someone might be able to answer with a number greater than 99, end numerical answers with an option that allows a higher number.

Incorrect: How many hats do you own?
- 0
- 1 to 4
- 5 to 9
- 10 to 99

Correct: How many hats do you own?
- 0
- 1 to 4
- 5 to 9
- 10 or more

Don't duplicate answers

If the answer options include 1 to 9 and 9 or more, what does someone choose if their answer is 9? Be careful that a number can't appear in more than one option.

Incorrect: How many pairs of shoes do you own?
- 0
- 1 to 9
- 9 or more

Correct: How many pairs of shoes do you own?
- 0
- 1 to 9
- 10 or more

Don't skip answers

Skipping numbers is a common problem particularly when every number appears in the answer list. The following example shows both a 5 and a 6 but what does someone choose if their answer is 6? Errors are less likely when every answer starts with a number.

Incorrect: How many packages of soup did you buy?
- 0
- 1 to 5
- More than 6

Correct: How many packages of soup did you buy?
- 0
- 1 to 5
- 6 or more

Use intuitive breaks

Before listing out frequency breaks, think about how often people do the thing being asked about. Is it a daily, weekly, monthly, or annual thing? Do people normally buy one, or two, or three at a time? If people think about certain things with a week as the backdrop, consider offering answer options that use a range of 7 to reflect the 7 days of the week.

In average week, about how many coffees do you buy at a coffee shop?
- 0
- 1 to 7
- 8 to 14
- 15 or more

In an average month, about how many times do you go grocery shopping?
- 0
- 1 to 4
- 5 to 8
- 9 to 12
- 13 or more

Use common breaks

People naturally think in 1s, 2s, 5s, and 10s. Don't break them out of that mode if you can avoid it. Choose common frequencies whenever possible:

In an average month, about how many books do you read?
- 0
- 1 or 2
- 3 or 4
- 5 or 6
- 7 or 8
- 9 or more

About how many boxes of cereal do you normally have in your cupboard?
- 0
- 1 to 4
- 5 to 9
- 10 to 14
- 15 or more

About how many pairs of shoes do you own?
- *0*
- *1 to 9*
- *10 to 19*
- *20 to 29*
- *30 to 39*
- *40 or more*

Play the misconstrue game

What's clear to you is often clear to someone else – in a very different way. With that in mind, go ask five people what this clear and unambiguous question means:

> *In an average month, about how many bottles of moisturizer does your household use?*

Option 1: It means that we use about half a bottle of moisturizer every month.

Option 2: It means that I keep a bottle in the bathroom, one in the living room, one in the bedroom, and one in the TV room. Thus, in an average month, I use four bottles of moisturizer.

Here is another example. How might someone misconstrue this question?

> *In an average month, how many packages of crackers do you eat?*

Option 1: I eat about 6 packages of crackers every month.

Option 2: I never eat the packages but I do recycle 6 packages every month after I eat the crackers inside.

It's extremely difficult to anticipate how every question might be legitimately misconstrued. Sometimes people are pedantic and sometimes they simply don't interpret your words the same way you do. This is exactly why you must pre-test every questionnaire and why you must never kick a record out of your dataset because of *one* invalid answer.

'Or' does not equal 'to'
When creating frequency ranges, use 'to' for things that can be counted in parts. Use 'or' for things that can only be counted in wholes.

In the first example below, by allowing someone to answer that they have 1 to 2 children, it is implied that they might have 1.5 children. It's not possible to have a partial child, a partial car, a partial store, a partial computer, or a partial hair cut (let's be realistic).

Incorrect: *How many children do you have?*
- *0*
- *1 to 2*
- *3 to 4*
- *5 or more*

Correct: *How many children do you have?*
- *0*
- *1 or 2*
- *3 or 4*
- *5 or more*

On the other hand, it is possible to use half of a bottle, one third of a can, one quarter of a package, or half of a container of something. It is acceptable to ask people if they use 1 or 2 bottles, but they might actually use 1.5 bottles. While the 'or' option is reasonable, it is not as good as the 'to' option.

Good: In an average month, how many packages of macaroni do you eat?
- 0
- 1 or 2
- 3 or 4
- 5 or more

Better: In an average month, how many packages of macaroni do you eat?
- 0
- 1 to 2
- 3 to 4
- 5 or more

Etc does not equal eg does not equal ie

Grammar doesn't need to be perfect but it also shouldn't be ignored.

- i.e., means 'in other words.' This acronym is used to reference one specific thing

- e.g., means 'for example.' This acronym is used at the beginning of a list of possible things.

- etc., means 'and other things" This acronym is used at the end of a list of possible things.

Never use e.g. and etc. in the same sentence. Further, if you choose to use e.g., use it consistently throughout the questionnaire rather than alternating with etc. For clarity, use e.g., rather than etc.

Incorrect: *Do you buy beverages? (e.g., juice, milk, water etc.)*
Correct: *Do you buy beverages? (e.g., juice, milk, water)*

Incorrect: *Do you buy beverages at restaurants?*
    (e.g., a place where people pay to sit and eat meals that are cooked and served on the premises)
Correct: *Do you buy beverages at restaurants?*
    (i.e., a place where people pay to sit and eat meals that are cooked and served on the premises)

Use your words

Dashes can be hard to read, easily misinterpreted, and completely unnoticed. Besides, dashes indicate subtraction. Do you want people to do math in the middle of the questionnaire? If the word 'to' or 'or' makes sense, use those instead of dashes.

With that in mind, go directly to your income and age questions and correct them.

Traditional: *What is your age?*
- *13 or under*
- *14-17*
- *18-29*
- *30-49*
- *50-69*
- *70 or over*

Better: *What is your age?*
- *13 or under*
- *14 to 17*
- *18 to 29*
- *30 to 49*
- *50 to 69*
- *70 or over*

Request estimates

Repeat after me again. People aren't robots. I don't know how many milliliters my rootbeer mug holds. I don't know how many bars of chocolate I ate last year. I can barely remember how many cans of tomatoes I bought on yesterday's grocery shopping trip.

While it is technically possible to ask people if they bought 1 or 2 or 3 or 7 cans of soup, doing so creates false precision. If that level of precision is essential, consider using a research methodology that incorporates loyalty cards or shopper data, something with physical records of purchases. Until then, ask people to remember things that they can remember. Use reasonable numbers and reasonable time frames. Use words that focus on estimates like 'about' and 'as best as you can recall.'

Unreasonable: How many cans of soup did you buy on your last grocery shopping trip?
- *0*
- *1*
- *2*
- *3*
- *4*
- *5*
- *6*
- *7 or more*

Better: About how many cans of soup did you buy on your last grocery shopping trip?
- *0*
- *1 to 3*
- *4 to 6*
- *7 or more*

Unreasonable: Over the last 12 months, how many cups of coffee did you drink (For this question, please consider one cup of coffee to be 250 milliliters)?

Better: In the last 24 hours, about how many cups of coffee did you drink?

Single-selects/Multi-selects

Single selects can be formatted either vertically or horizontally. While both look fine on a large screen, only vertical formats work well on small devices. For the sake of consistency across both small and large screens, choose a vertical format.

Traditional: What is your opinion about eating chocolate for breakfast?

Love	Like	Neutral	Dislike	Hate
o	o	o	o	o

Better: What is your opinion about eating chocolate for breakfast?
- *Love*
- *Like*
- *Neutral*
- *Dislike*
- *Hate*

Continuing with the mobile frame of mind and the need to avoid scrolling, although fifty brands can be listed in a brand awareness question, it is never ideal. When a long list looms ahead, use as few answer options as possible, and focus on the ones that *must* be included.

There is no set rule about how many answer options is too many but for a simply worded question with short answer options, up to twenty answer options can likely be used without creating an overly negative impact on people and the data.

Scales

Scales don't reveal truth
One of the most important things to remember when writing scales is that no matter how carefully the scale is prepared, there is often no externally true and confirmable answer. People interpret emotional and perceptual scales in personal ways, and try to squish themselves in sets of answers that don't precisely reflect their unique life experiences.

Scales might read precisely and you might be able to generate lots of decimal places with the data but it is manufactured precision. Prepare scales knowing that the results are valid but not in the same way that purchase or behavioural data is valid.

Number of points
As a general rule, aim for five-point scales and avoid using scales with more than seven points. Anything greater than that creates false precision.

Once you've decided whether you're going to use a 4, ,5 ,6 or 7-point scale, be consistent across the entire questionnaire. Sometimes it may be necessary to use scales with more than 7 points but this should be a rare and avoided occurrence.

Balanced scales
Scales should be balanced so that people are not led towards positive or negative answers. With a five-point scale, aim to have two answer options that are positive, two negative, and one neutral.

What is your opinion about this statement?
I like to try new things.
- o *Agree strongly*
- o *Agree somewhat*
- o *Neutral*
- o *Disagree somewhat*
- o *Disagree strongly*

Unbalanced scales

In rare circumstances, unbalanced scales might be appropriate. If previous data shows that more than 90% of people feel positively (or negatively) about the thing being measured, the negative (or positive) side of the scale would be wasted. A five-point scale would be effectively reduced to a two-point scale.

By changing one negative answer to a positive answer, the distribution or spread of the answers can be increased, allowing for better data analysis. Thus, rather than seeing 90% of the answers spread across two positive answer options, those answers would spread across three positive options.

Rarely better: *What is your opinion about this statement? Wifi should be free in public spaces.*
- o *Agree strongly*
- o *Agree somewhat*
- o *Agree slightly*
- o *Neutral*
- o *Disagree*

Midpoints

Researchers don't always agree on the use of midpoints, but if we consider them from the perspective of people answering questionnaires, including midpoints should be the default. People want midpoints and that desire should be respected.

If you have a fantastic reason for not using midpoints, do so sparingly. For instance, if you are trying to predict something that has a behaviorally measurable yes/no outcome (e.g., an election), using a 4-point or 6-point scale can force people to lean towards a yes or no.

Caution is necessary with the use of midpoints. People interpret midpoints in a variety of ways including Not Applicable, Don't know, Neutral, Can't decide, Neither, and Other. Keep these in mind when preparing scales. Consider whether it is essential to provide one of these options separately so that a Not Applicable answer is not confused with a Neutral answer.

Traditional: Thinking about the claims of HealthyHands lotion, what is your opinion about these statements?

	Agree Strongly	Agree Somewhat	Neutral	Disagree	Disagree Somewhat	Don't Know Strongly
New	○	○	○	○	○	○
Different	○	○	○	○	○	○
Believable	○	○	○	○	○	○
Likeable	○	○	○	○	○	○

Scale labels

Labeling every point on a scale generates better quality data because people are more likely to interpret the answer options in a similar way.

Weak: *Chocolate is a good choice for breakfast.*
   ○   *5 Agree strongly*
   ○   *4*
   ○   *3*
   ○   *2*
   ○   *1 Disagree strongly*

Better: *Chocolate is a good choice for breakfast.*
- *Agree strongly*
- *Agree somewhat*
- *Neutral*
- *Disagree somewhat*
- *Disagree strongly*

Grid/matrix questions

Deconstruct grids

Grid questions require every item to use the same scale answers. However, deconstructed grids can use scales that reflect the unique content of each item. This adds variety and interest to the questionnaire. And, they work much better on small screens.

Traditional: *Thinking about the product description for HealthyHands, what is your opinion about these statements?*

	Agree Strongly	Agree Somewhat	Neutral	Disagree Somewhat	Disagree Strongly
New	o	o	o	o	o
Different	o	o	o	o	o

Deconstructed: *Thinking about the product description, how would you rate HealthyHands?*
- *Extremely new*
- *Very new*
- *Somewhat new*
- *Slightly new*
- *Not new at all*

Deconstructed: *Thinking about the product description, how would you rate HealthyHands?*
- *Extremely different*
- *Very different*
- *Somewhat different*
- *Slightly different*
- *Not different at all*

If the questionnaire software does not automatically deconstruct grid questions into individual questions, do not write grid questions. Instead, write a series of individual single-select questions as in the examples.

Choose few grid items
If a grid question will be presented properly on a small screen, either because the software will deconstruct it or because the grid will only show if the person is using a large screen, design the grid with no more than eight items. Any more and readers will become annoyed and data quality will suffer.

If a grid must have more than eight items, cut the grid into more than one question. For example, a grid that reflects both emotional ratings and product features could be broken into two separate grids about those two topic areas.

Create reverse keyed items
The most effective grid questions use an equal number of both standard and reverse keyed items. It's hard for brand and product managers to acknowledge the negative aspects of products and services they're so proud of, and it's even harder to suggest those negative aspects to the people answering our questionnaires. But it must be done.

Including reverse keyed (negative) items encourages people to thoroughly read and think about every item. And, it allows researchers to properly measure data quality through straightlining. If you care about data quality, you must create reverse/negative keyed items.

Create negative items

When constructing negative items to meet the need for reverse keyed items, avoid 'not' words. Avoid aren't, can't, couldn't, didn't, doesn't, don't, isn't, never, no, shouldn't, won't, wouldn't, and, of course, not. These words are more difficult to interpret and can be easily missed during the reading process. Focus on using opposite words rather than negative words. Search online for an antonym dictionary to make your life easier.

I don't like this brand.	→ *I hate this brand.*
This cereal doesn't taste good.	→ *This cereal tastes bland.*
The box isn't attractive.	→ *The box is ugly.*
The price isn't good.	→ *The price is expensive.*
The store wasn't clean.	→ *The store was dirty.*
The cashiers weren't friendly.	→ *The cashiers were rude.*

Instructions

Traditional grids using agreement or importance scales that are familiar to people won't necessarily need instructions. However, scales that are unusual or grids that need vertical selections might necessitate instructions.

Please select one answer in each row.
Please select one answer in each column.
Select answers in every row and column that apply to you.

Rank questions

Questionnaires aren't math tests nor intelligence tests. Keeping the need for high data quality in mind, only ask people to rank up to five items. If the questionnaire software uses a drag and drop feature (which probably won't generate a good user experience on a small device), it might be possible to include up to eight items without annoying readers. Use appropriate instructions such as:

Please drag and drop the answers so that the answer you like the most is at the top, and the answer you like the least is at the bottom.

Please rank the answers from 1 through 5. 1 means you like it the most and 5 means you like it the least. Please use each number only once.

Sum questions

Don't ask people to sum more than five items. Any more than that constitutes increased cognitive load and will encourage response fatigue. Don't make people work too hard if you want high quality data.

If automated validation isn't used, perhaps because the question is a data quality measure, expect that the answers will not add up to the desired sum. This is okay because, well, people aren't robots. Math might not be hard for you, but it is for other people. Use an appropriate instruction such as:

Please make sure your numbers add up to 100%

Other (Please specify)

If you have no intention of reading and acting on every response to a 'Please specify' question, do not require people to specify their answer. People generally don't enjoy writing answers on questionnaires, so requiring them to do this five or ten or fifteen times is unreasonable. People agreed in advance to click boxes, not write essays.

If knowing the specific answer isn't imperative, simply use 'Other' and allow them to continue with the questionnaire.

Short text

If people must be asked to write or type answers, phrase the question in such a way that people know short answers are appropriate.

What one thing did you like the least about HealthyHands?
Who recommended HealthyHands to you?

Long text

If reading the words and understanding the word choice of consumers is important, cut those components from the questionnaire and use qualitative methods instead. People who agreed to complete questionnaires agreed to click in boxes, not provide essay style answers. Make sure the task you ask people to do is the task they signed up for.

That said, there is nothing wrong with asking people to answer a couple of longer text questions. Give them some guidance though. Avoid generic, broad requests and instead ask for specific answers.

Avoid questions that can be answered with a yes or no such as:

Do you like the packaging?
Have you used the product in an unusual way?
Would you use this product?

Instead, use questions that incorporate who, what, where, when, why, and how. Other good options include 'tell me,' 'explain,' 'list,' 'describe,' and 'name three.'

What three things did you like about HealthyHands?
Please describe how you use HealthyHands in a typical day.
What one thing would you change about the packaging?

Chapter 7: Sensitive Questions

Don't assign negativity

You might look at people who are different and feel empathy or pity towards them but those emotions belong to you, not the other person. Don't let your personal feelings transfer to your question wording. You don't *know* if people are suffering or unhappy, and you certainly don't want to make them think they ought to suffer or feel unhappy. Instead, choose neutral and unassuming words.

Traditional: Are you confined to a wheelchair?
Traditional: Do you benefit from a wheelchair?
Better: Do you use a wheelchair?

Traditional: Which of these do you suffer from?
- ☐ Asthma
- ☐ Arthritis
- ☐ Diabetes

Better: Which of these do you have?
- ☐ Asthma
- ☐ Arthritis
- ☐ Diabetes

Traditional: Do you complain of discomfort?
Better: Do you have discomfort?

Traditional: Were you fortunate to have a child this year?
Better: Did you have a child this year?

Traditional: Where did you enjoy your holidays last year?
Better: Where did you go on holidays last year?

Socially undesirable behaviours

It can be embarrassing to admit doing something that isn't nice. Give people legitimate explanations that will make them feel more comfortable providing a valid answer.

We understand this topic might be difficult to talk about. However, your opinions will help shape and improve public policy so that people will be better served in the future.

Second, use leading questions for good. If you expect people will underreport a behaviour because they are embarrassed, give them legitimate reasons to admit to the behavior. And, include some neutral answers to give a more impartial perspective to the topic.

Even though some people want to vote, they aren't always able to. Were you able to vote in the last election?
- o   *Yes, I was able to vote*
- o   *No, I couldn't get a ride*
- o   *No, I couldn't find a caregiver*
- o   *No, I couldn't get time off work*
- o   *No, I didn't like any of the candidates*
- o   *No, other reason*
- o   *Don't recall*

Sometimes, when you've had a difficult few days at work, it's hard to be as polite as you normally like to be. Have you done any of these things in the last week?
- ☐   *Didn't hold the door open for someone*
- ☐   *Smoked in a no-smoking area*
- ☐   *Didn't stay late when I probably should have*
- ☐   *Took a longer lunch break than I should have*
- ☐   *Didn't answer my phone when it was ringing*
- ☐   *Don't recall*
- ☐   *Didn't do any of these*

Finally, be sure to include an opt-out answer such as 'Don't recall' or 'Prefer not to answer,' especially if none of the alternative answers are neutral enough.

Illegal activities

This is where I love to take advantage of human biases. Confessing to illegal activities on questionnaires is difficult even though we know the answers are anonymous. However, researchers can frame these questions so that people feel more comfortable providing honest answers. Normalize the behaviour or put it in a context where the behavior is common, so that it appears to be not much worse than other questionable behaviours that lots of people do.

Which of these have you done?
- ☐ *Didn't tell a cashier they gave me too much change*
- ☐ *Borrowed someone's pen and didn't return it*
- ☐ *Drove more than ten kilometers over the speed limit*
- ☐ *Fell asleep at the wheel*
- ☐ *Had too much to drink but drove home anyways*
- ☐ *Didn't hold the door open for someone*
- ☐ *Took a soda that did not belong to me*

Chapter 8: Demographics

It doesn't matter whether you believe in these recommendations but it does matter that you understand the reasoning behind them and respect the people who will answer the questions. Respect is the only way to generate high completion rates and high quality data.

Most questionnaires include at least age, gender, and region. Depending the research needs, additional variables could include: race/ethnicity, household size, number and age of children, education, income, religion, and language.

Demographic questions can feel overly personal so be sure to include 'Prefer not to answer' as an option. Data quality will suffer less from having no answer as opposed to deliberately incorrect answers.

Gender/Sex
It is no longer appropriate to offer only two answer options. Though the percentage is tiny, some people don't feel that a binary male/female choice reflects their situation.

Further, the words sex and gender mean different things. You cannot substitute one for the other. If there is no specific reason to use one term, consider using neither.

For much of marketing research, there is no reason to specify sex or gender.

Traditional:	*What is your sex?*
Traditional:	*What is your gender?*
Better:	*Which option describes you?*
Better:	*Are you...?*

Best: *Which of these describes you?*
- *Female*
- *Male*
- *Other*
- *Prefer not to answer*

If you're conducting medical or pharmaceutical research, research related to hormones, reproductivity, or similar types of topics, you will naturally want to specify sex. But it is particularly important that you couch the question with appropriate explanations so that people can fully understand why you must know this exact personal information.

Do keep in mind, however, that some groups of people might be offended by this type of language. Before boldly going forth with this new language, be aware of whether the target group could have a negative reaction to it.

Age

The definition of a child differs in every country by law and by association guidelines. You must respect *both* requirements. If the legal definition of a child is 17 and under, but the industry definition is 14 and under, incorporate those two cut-off points into the answer options. Don't end up in a situation where permission wasn't obtained for a 14-year-old because the age question measured '13 and under.'

Matching words

If the age answer options specify 13 or under, then specify 70 or over. On the other hand, if the answer options specify 13 or younger, then match the phrasing by specifying 70 or older. I recommend using the under and over options to avoid the negative connotation associated with the word 'older.' Also, depending on the questionnaire topic, consider being a little cheeky and asking people if they are '70 or better.'

People don't want to feel old
As much as we'd like people be proud of their life experience, many people don't want to feel old. And this leads to data inaccuracies. Where possible, include extra answer options at the beginning and the end of the age breaks. This gives older people room to fudge a tiny bit younger without unduly affecting the validity of the data. Similarly, for younger people who feel like they'll be excluded if they aren't legally an adult, it gives them room to fudge a tiny bit older.

No, people shouldn't lie about their age but they also shouldn't eat an entire bag of cookies in one sitting. Not that I have. Not today. This is the reality of the human being so accept people for who and what they are.

Which age group includes you?
- *9 or under*
- *10 to 14*
- *15 to 17*
- *18 to 29*
- *30 to 39*
- *40 to 49*
- *50 to 59*
- *60 to 69*
- *70 to 79*
- *80 or better*

Race/Ethnicity
Similar to gender/sex, there is often no need to introduce confusion by using the word race or ethnicity. Avoid the issue by using neither word.

Also, use a multi-select format so that people can choose the set of options that applies best to them. If you really need to, you can always segment people into the desired groups afterwards, during the analysis stage.

Traditional: *What race are you?*
Traditional: *What ethnicity are you?*
Better: *Which of these describe you?*

Education

Don't equate more degrees with being better educated. During the five or ten years you were siloed in a college or university, other people were gaining five or ten years of highly relevant job and life experience. It helps no one if people finish questionnaires on a low note so avoid terms like highest or most. People know what you mean and they'll give you the right answer without those words.

Traditional: *What is the highest level of education you have received?*
Traditional: *What is the most education you have received?*
Traditional: *What is your highest educational accomplishment?*

Better: *Which one describes the education you have completed?*
- *Public School*
- *High School degree*
- *College Certificate or Diploma*
- *Bachelor's degree*
- *Master's degree*
- *Doctorate or equivalent*

Employment

The employment question should be asked as a multi-select. People have complicated lives and it is completely reasonable for someone who works full-time to also have a part-time job, go to school part-time, and care for their elderly parents. Use the data analysis process to choose which people belong in a particular analysis.

Further, be respectful of changing family roles. Caregivers aren't just mothers of small children. Caregivers are men and women who look after babies, foster children, adult children, parents, grandparents, cousins, and people who aren't related by legal status. Avoid the phrases Stay-At-Home Mom and Stay-At-Home Dad and focus on Caregivers. Similarly, avoid the words Housewife and Househusband and focus on Homemaker or something similar.

Which of these describe you?
- ☐ *Full-time employed*
- ☐ *Part-time employed*
- ☐ *Not employed (e.g., retired, unable to work, looking for work)*
- ☐ *Caregiver*
- ☐ *Homemaker*
- ☐ *Full-time student*
- ☐ *Part-time student*
- ☐ *Other*

Children

Consider whether children must belong to the person answering the questionnaire or simply be in the home. Grandparents, adult children, and even non-relatives may have significant responsibilities for shopping, caregiving, feeding, and selecting entertainment for children.

Necessary?	*How many children do you have?*
Sufficient?	*How many children live in your home?*
Sufficient?	*How many children do you care for?*

Chapter 9: Tidbits

Branding a questionnaire
Because of unconscious cueing, using brand colours as part of questionnaire design can significantly affect the outcome of research, and change scores.

Do not use any branding features if you plan to measure brand recall, awareness, purchase, attitudes, or perceptions, particularly if you want to compare with competitive brands. Questionnaire formatting should be neutral in all ways such that unconscientious recollections won't be created.

If you're not sure if branding would be ok, don't do it at all. Better safe than sorry.

Questions per page
Many questionnaire software programs default to one question per page. This style works well on questionnaires taken on smaller devices but it is not essential. In some cases, questions that are similar to each might best be presented on one page. For example, when a grid is deconstructed, those few questions might be presented well on a single page.

Pretesting
You've worked hard to prepare your masterpiece so don't waste your efforts. Pretest it first with several colleagues. Encourage them to find typos and logic mistakes. Encourage them to misinterpret words. Find mistakes before you launch.

Next, try some cognitive interviews and probe people to learn why they did or didn't choose certain answers.

Then, pretest the questionnaire with at least ten people, some of whom are in the target group and some who are not. This will help ensure that every question has appropriate substantive answer options and opt-outs. Figure out which questions had no variation among the answers and refine them.

Email subject lines
Avoid specifying the questionnaire topic in the email subject line and anywhere else in an email invitation as this can cause several problems.

◆ Incidence rates might be over-estimated because people who are not interested in the topic may choose to not participate.
◆ Incidence rates might be over-estimated because people who feel they have sufficient (but not precisely relevant) information about that topic might want to feel included.
◆ You may be unable to learn why people don't use a category because they self-select out once they read the topic and realize it's not something they use/do/buy/eat.

Poor: *Answer a fun survey about aluminum rims!*
Poor: *Great survey for car fans!*

Better: *Share your opinions in this survey!*
Better: *Make your opinion heard in this consumer survey*

If your target group is avid category users and you don't need to learn incidence rates or why people don't use your category, this could be less of a concern.

In most cases however, it is wise to not mention the questionnaire topic until the point where you have absolutely no alternative but to do so.

Reminders

Although you call them reminders, many people call them annoying. People might deliberately ignore reminders because the incentive isn't enticing, they no longer have the time, or they are no longer interested in completing surveys for you. Be respectful of people and send no more than two or three reminders. After that point, those emails will become more annoying, and less reminding.

Reveal the results

I'm willing to bet that not every single question in your survey will generate proprietary information that absolutely cannot be shared with anyone. Pick a few questions out of your questionnaire and show the results to the people who shared their opinions with you. It hurts you none and the people who took ten or twenty minutes out of their day deserve to know more about the project they just participated in.

About the Author

Annie Pettit, PhD, is a Fellow of the Marketing Research and Intelligence Association, the Canadian body for market research. She received a PhD in experimental psychology after completing her dissertation on the data quality of offline and online surveys. She became a certified Industrial Organizational Psychologist in 2000 (certification not maintained). Annie has more than twenty years of experience writing, analyzing, advising, and teaching questionnaire design in the professional world of marketing research. She writes for professional journals and industry associations and has been an invited speaker at many industry conferences. She won a 2016 Ginny Valentine Award, 2014 ESOMAR Excellence Award for Best Paper, 2014 MRIA Award of Outstanding Merit, 2013 ESOMAR award for Best Methodological Paper, and the 2011 David K. Hardin Award. Her first book published in 2011, The Listen Lady, is a novel about social media research. She is also the author of "7 Strategies and 10 Tactics to Become a Thought Leader." All three books are available on Amazon.

Twitter: @LoveStats
LinkedIn: https://ca.linkedin.com/in/anniepettit

Made in the USA
Coppell, TX
08 September 2021